Where the Moss Grows Old

Madelyn Rose Craig

Rosewood Publishing

Copyright © 2021 by Madelyn Rose Craig.

All rights reserved. No part of this publication may be reproduced, distributed, or transmitted in any form or by any means, including photocopying, recording, or other electronic or mechanical methods, without the prior written permission of the author, except in the case of brief quotations embodied in critical reviews and certain other noncommercial uses permitted by copyright law.

ISBN: 978-1-7355711-2-6 (Paperback)
ASIN: B09NL9LDQV (Kindle)

LCCN: 2021925204

Rosewood Publishing
www.madelynrosecraig.com

Contents

Wonder 1

    Before I Forget 3

    A Snow Globe World 4

    Horsefeathers 5

    The Hummingbird 6

    Story from a Bird.....................................7

    Frost 8

    Garden Moments 9

    Who Am I...10

    Postal Hue..12

    Secret Friends 13

    Morning 14

    Dew Drops...15

    Frosted Nights 16

    Sunlight 17

    A Walk Through the Forest...................18

    Hope from a Messenger 20

    The Star Date...21

    August 22

    Morning Shade 23

    Winter First..24

    The Yew Tree 25

    Nightwalk 27

Memory **29**
   The Invisible 31
   The Introvert 32
   The Toy Box 33
   Lost 34
   Secrets 35
   About Time 36
   The Love Story 37
   "Between you and I" 39
   Veritas 41
   A Cry from a Lonely Heart 42
   The Bracelet 44
   One Question 46
   Understanding 47
   Cloudy Thoughts 49
   Sleepwalk 50
   Numb 51
   The Flicker of the Candle 52
   Bottle Up My Tears 53
   Drops Like Blood 54
   Scars 55
   New Song 56
   Tiny Treasures 57
   Sleep 58
   From Clouds to Light 59

Home 61
    Autumn 63

    Seasons 64

    Gifts and Thanks 66

    Lessons 67

    Prayers 69

    Thoughts of Remembrance 70

    April Nights 71

    Just Because 72

    Day One 73

    The Wall 74

    …and then I met you 76

    My Poem 77

    Moondance 78

    Red Nights 79

    Twined Souls 80

    Inkhorn Mornings 81

    Animated Lines 82

    This Old House 83

    Church Bells 85

    Little One 86

    New Life 88

    Grace 89

    Midnight Visits 92

    Last Night's Waking 93

About the Author 97

Wonder

Before I Forget

Treading soft on forest bare
little feet are found in air
so that the eye
may choose to lie
upon the mossy ground

There a secret may be kept
past the hour this time has swept
where mem'ry sleeps
until one keeps
the wonder of what's found

Think not of what is and naught
but only the moment sought
where ag'ed prime
can keep the time
when we are young within

For the moss grows back anew
painting heartbeats, secrets true
and then you'll find
between your mind
a mem'ry yours again

A Snow Globe World

Gaze upon this snow globe world;
This wondrous beauty, see!
Countless stars of crystal lace
Fallen on you and me.

Through the glazed trees, I watch
A light shine through a glass,
Prisms upon blanket white,
Swelling with dell and pass.

The trees share this splendor fair,
A shawl upon each bough.
Don't reach to touch their cool silk;
Your pane doth not allow.

I look once more on this frail paint,
Though hindered by the glass,
The crystals lighting on my view
Like feathers on the grass.

And as we leave this fading world—
The sun makes none endure—
I know He gives each season
Until the world's made pure.

Horsefeathers

On days that run with chills and drafts,
Warmed with the summer rays,
A freckled face runs out and laughs
To embrace running days.
For as the spring turned winter warm
The ground made green again
Her steed, ancy to brace the storm,
Was glad to see her grin.

Summer days have much delight,
Though few come quite like this,
To find a day so clear and bright
With each surface sun kissed.
Then up she went, the shiny back,
And brushed as though made new,
To make it quickly to the track
Which gleam'ed with the dew.

Across the hills' fresh amber grass,
They raced the day away;
Before they knew the time to pass,
The moon was on its way.
As one they went with tired trots
And both to each their home;
Their sleep was filled with happy thoughts
Of each new hill to roam.

The Hummingbird

Flutter here, and whisper there,
Sing a song for one;
Hum a merry little tune
Winging in the sun.

Pretty flowers catch the glow
Of rays, sparkling light,
Atop the crisp, dew'ed grass,
Of little feather's flight.

Twitt'rings pass the hours of day,
A nose nests in bloom;
Two pearly stones hide away
In home like a tomb.

No breeze stirs our feather fair,
Though so small is she,
For beady eyes guide rubies
'Round gems pure and free.

Then night steals the day so fast
When her frets must cease;
Nestled in her home, at last,
The feather finds peace.

Story from a Bird

Broken wings are healed at last,
And birds begin to sing;
A heart smiles, a glance is cast
With all the joy they bring.

Melodies on tattered heart,
What's broken mends for sure;
Like birds gathered once apart,
The freedom was the cure.

A key, a heart, little house,
The door was melded shut
'Til heavy wings lift'd to rouse
That room and flittered out.

When at last came long lost date,
Away they flew their cage;
The door stood open to wait
For hands to turn the page.

Frost

Slowly comes this faint touch,
One hardly seen or felt;
Hands so soft, color lost,
And on the grass it knelt.
Here, little teardrops fell,
Though life and joy they brought;
Petals gleamed and glistened—
Such diamonds can't be bought.
This little display held
These little teardrops mine,
Caught fast on edges green,
With rainbow lights they shine.
Gaze now to fragile glass
On blades near glossy stream;
Find joy in minute hues—
Much brighter now they seem.
And as warmth enclos'ed cold,
The teardrops gleamed and passed.
Lowly diamonds faded,
Their life was none to last.
Here no more, they'll return
To greet me morning's rise,
Then hasten to heaven's door,
And leave with twinkling eyes.

Garden Moments

Betwixt meadows and mossy paths,
Stood trees as close as kin
Where thorns and thistles grow
And stories met again.

Yea, long ago when young the dew,
And ancient was new birth,
Stood lonely untouched bud
With subtle hints of mirth.

What joy! But wait a moment now;
Before its time had come,
Hands of a passerby
Tore harsh the petal from.

Afraid and hurt as darkness fell,
Unsure who treaded paths,
Moss and grass grew a fence
'Round where our flower sat.

Ancient comes as ancient goes,
Feared was the morn to come
'Til star-shown crystaled tips
The tears of heaven wrung.

Thus ends our tale of joy to woe,
Crossed love was not to last;
Roses stained with love's lips
On petals, dead, now cast.

Who Am I

A port within my name resides
The brightest rainbow new
In mirrors of some rippled glass
And eyes of someone true
Forget me not, I'm always there
Here spread across a sky
Even in bows of windblown hair
And feathered bird on high
I can be seen in many ways
Though seldom I am heard
Nighttime whispers my fading glow
Ask the snowflakes' small word
A stone, mirror, and looking glass
Reflects myself in panes
Flower petals and dew dropped grass
Hidden in seashells' veins
I'm the color of midnight sun
A tip of crashing wave
Reflecting the deep down below
And crystals in a cave
I am what a life's waters fill
And what wonders I hold
Yet I can make one to be still
When darkness brings the cold
I dance light in butterfly winds
Gently I sway the pine
The raindrops on a mirror lake
Are filled with shades of mine
The darkness of a mountainside
And clouds reflect my glow

If only you would then abide
When always I am shown
Be patient in those morning rays
You'll see me standing there
Though this mist may rouse me darkened
A beauty I will share
So come whisper in the moonlight
The stars won't hide the deeps
My shades will reach from the vast heights
To depths where anchor sleeps

Postal Hue

A little girl of portal blue
Gazes fondly at the start
Darkness quick
Surrounds her thick
But eyes reflect the heart

Secret Friends

When I was a little girl
I had a little friend
Her name was lily rose
And she lived inside my head

We once talked of secret things
That only two could know
Reflecting the other
Where I traveled she would go

Laughter or a singing tune
Our voice would fill the sky
And when the storm clouds came
On my own shoulder she'd cry

Sometimes she told echoed past
Or fears of yet to come
And whispered little things
That never could be undone

Yet this friend left me one day
To life I've yet not known
Wonder I of those days
And whether she has yet grown

Morning

waking up the moonlit night
the stars flicker candlelight
on feathered crystals all around
and silence is the only sound

Dew Drops

water with light pass
    shining off its frame
early in the morning,
    while the air is cool
before the day's heat
    steals away its glimmer
with reflections of the world 'round
    upside down, miniscule
bent, imperfect...
    but a mirror same
little rainbows, tears,
    and broken glass.

Frosted Nights

Frosty winter moonlit walk
Silent little glances talk
Hands are held tight once again
Sheltered from all life's sharp wind
Kept so close in fear of frost
Never again will I be lost

Sunlight

filtering through leaves,
          golden beams
brightness sifting deepest thought,
             wakened dreams
peaceful, coming down like dew,
              teardrops shine
graceful, swirling round with ease,
                keeping time
slowly green and blue gaze meet,
                  now kept still
weaving through curtained tops and
                    'round boughs spill

A Walk Through the Forest

I walked alone the garden
Beside the bushes bare
Dancing upon the flowers
With sunlight in my hair.

Glancing down at rose petals,
A tear rolled from my eye,
Before I looked to see that
The sky had come to cry.

Away from tears and sadness,
I ran from the deep sky
To where no one could then see
How empty now was I.

Watching the trees shake fearful,
The flowers stood the wind;
But I just barely standing
To take the rounding bend.

Hidden with cloak of treetops,
Small lace now glistened wet,
Trying to recall the songs
Of birds that we once met.

But no, the waves are grim here;
Here, things lost are not found.
Naught is sure to be over;
All wand'rers will lose ground.

The rain slowed down its descent
As the sun dried its eyes,
And I began to see then
That lakes take empty skies.

Wond'ring at this great passion,
How sadness, aching, pain
Can bring joy to the morning,
Can grow flowers in rain.

I walk alone the garden,
My heart heavy at best,
But dew dries in the daylight,
And clouds never do last.

My past, my fears mistake me
As someone too far gone;
But as the sun brings morning,
So rain washes like song.

I walk alone the garden
In hand with what's to be;
A new rose now is growing
With hands by rain made free.

Hope from a Messenger

Darkness crept 'round bends and turns,
A pathway lit by stars,
Hilly roads to crouching paths—
Their journey brought them far.

Before on a hidden path,
Lay stories to be told:
Of secrets kept, travels made,
And dreams that we can hold.

Crystals formed where dewdrops stood;
The stars from heaven fell.
One would speak who never could,
And all was left to tell.

Below a hill, between trees,
Lay sanctuary dark.
Wherever these trav'lers go
From here, they'll never part.

Wearied then, they lay to see
What host shone bright to soothe.
Whispers made for some to hear
When stars forbade them move.

Yet nighttime called quick to them,
Long after clock struck twelve;
Starry letters brought hope lost,
And again, this silly thing, love.

The Star Date

Long days and
Misty haze stand,
Summer nights with
Lasting lights swift,
Times fly while
Years die in miles,
With lives that pass
And moments that last,
While dreaming here
With you, my dear.

August

Lie in grass like earthenware
Let earthly crawlers through your hair
And gaze at rusted evergreens
As sun remains in clouds unseen

Morning Shade

The vocals gather before robin's song
Like shrouded cloak, mist coats us all
Waiting, the sun's not drank earth's light
And I, hair damp, eyes dry, now watch
The morning gain its pastel hue

The world is silhouette, uncolored
Trees disappear into the gray
Yet I, alive, feel cold and pale
For the sun still hides her spark

I pause, a bird to stretch her breast
A note comes out a sigh, and yet
The world hears in deafness, a waste
While the morning dries her tears

Whispers of hue alight the hanging drops
In the air, a frost suspended, and
I fade with it into the sun
For as I go, the colors come

Winter First

Frigid glass meets my tiny hand,
Frost on the pane, the sill a purer white.
Fragile pictures paint the perfect land,
Fans of rainbow stain and crystal light.

Swirling, news comes in little drifts;
Soft, unrushed in your frantic haste.
Song of yours through hollow cliffs;
Still, so fast laid on frozen place.

I reach to touch the flakey dew, now cool,
Ingrained with image none can repeat.
Inhale, out, my breath like tule
In the frosted land, a silken sheet.

E'en though the sun comes high at noon,
Each fragile dew won't leave me soon.

The Yew Tree

The Yew tree stood there somber,
In the shade of evening light,
And I gazed upon the frame
Of an everlasting sight.

The mighty branches ponder
As they hold upon its frame
The doorposts of the churchyard
And the eons of its name.

For hills had watched your growing
And the echoed walls within,
Where multitudes of mem'ries
Flocked from matins to compline.

Your figure never wavered
From a sapling to your youth
In the ways the people found
Many uses, some uncouth.

Though your boughs brought them shelter,
Some would tear them from their sheath
For shooting many swift darts,
Their homes buried underneath.

Yet your heart was warm'ed red
With a blood of purest white,
Reflecting their communion,
Your branches would portal right.

My holy Yew, I wonder,
As I stare upon your bough,
If God formed you in concord
Where you grow so firmly now?

To the stone of your altar,
That your roots do now embrace,
And your boughs grasp so tightly,
Like an everlasting race.

Melded now, both branch and bark,
To a portal made of stone;
Death and life, forever made
A firm hearth where He atone.

Yet I know your days are few,
Though their number, I know not;
I walk now inside your heart
And behold both time and rot.

But I can see your future,
My dear everlasting Yew;
As you take your final bough,
You then start a life anew.

Nightwalk

I've become a friend with the night
Betwixt the flick of candlelight
After the sun goes out of sight
And the moon shows its marv'lous light

When mem'ries wander through the trees
And flowers close for lack of bees
With widened pupils all to seize
And shades of blue are on the breeze

Of softened touch on gentle grass
As winds whisper and 'round me pass
A heart can make a skittish lass
When walking though the forming glass

I sneak between the hedge and ferns
To find from what the night now learns
Of a girl who adventure yearns
And as she came, then back she turns

The stars they glitter evermore
Before the sun and on the shore
On waves of grass from hev'ns door
When night brings forth the tales of lore

The dews come out at time of sleep
When the little mice and owls peep
When what I find is mine to keep
That's when at night I love to creep

But nighttime ends as good things do
And sun will rise again anew
The sky will fade from black to blue
And that's when I'll return to you

Now nothing can bring me to fright
When I am firmly out of sight
After the shadows hide their light
My secret friend will be the night

Memory

The Invisible

Hush, now, and invisible see
Ethereal thought between future dream,
Times to come in moments now
Resting lightly on your brow.

Moments pass through flashes then
While waiting for the frozen moment when
Starshined moonlight filters through.
Where gazes meet? Here they do.

Patience now, though slowly come;
These teardrops must wait, but here only from
Lasting promise, love that's kept.
On these thoughts, I fin'ly slept.

The Introvert

A quiet world of constant sound,
Thoughts drift on for miles.
A candled place to be found,
And silent are the smiles.

Endless paths of days and years;
A touch of each sensation.
The world wonders at frozen tears;
Nothing, yet such emotion.

Penciled words on moonlit leaves,
A vibrant hand emotes.
A crystal view, and muddled griefs,
The creator's mind here dotes.

People pass this little light,
Silent a garden's grown
Of thoughts and words—this sight!—
And only when sought, is shown.

The Toy Box

I thought that if they left my sight,
That mem'ries could live in things,
A toy'd regain its plastic form,
And cut glass from diamond rings.

I thought that in a hidden box,
And away from probing minds,
The pressured rock would turn cement,
And my heart could loose its binds.

I thought that as from box to bag,
My hands could then lose their touch,
That felts and silks would loosen threads,
And each bead would roll as such.

But my heart knew what eyes ignored,
While old hands silently shook
As crumbled leaves and long dead flowers,
Their resting place they forsook.

For glass, paper are ending things,
And for a child that is still;
While one may live in hearts and minds,
These take hands with renewed will.

Lost

Muddled moments blind the thought
with fear to shroud the day,
empty, shaking boughs now caught
what's left of springtime's day.

Whisper quickly, watch the hour
before this leaf lies dead;
creeping silent, chill and cower,
and freeze the flower's bed.

Settle heartbeats with the dawn,
or wait until the chime;
filling closing hands soon gone,
and keep heart's life to shine.

Secrets

Time ends when day's still young
and questions yet remain.
A crying heart and broken song
on crumpled bed are lain.
What's the secret that's carefully made?

Redding spheres of crystal glass
begin to shed their drops
of memories that long since passed
when it suddenly stopped.
It has always been there, but never said.

Listless, wander forest bare—
a bud withers and dies—
until someone comes by to share
a hand and really tries.
For while there was speaking, it silent bled.

Days melt like snowy eve,
and dances end at nigh.
Ye, hearts will never truly leave,
and never say goodbye.
Softly caress the beauty that stayed.

About Time

The seasons pass like blossom dead,
And days end soon with clouds;
Yet I, so still with paper, pen,
Watch time as business shrouds.

For time is quite a silly thing—
I sit with simple thought—
While the birds take leave umprompted,
As if time's here, and naught.

Yet well I know time goes too fast—
I know this more than most—
That speeding up to meet the stop,
Meets regret at the post.

I wish, truly, to love what I do,
And do what I love well;
But as I watch past's restless ways
I despise 'fore they tell.

And yet I hold the time I have,
The cygnet hidden gray,
With hope that in a little time
Beauty will show someday.

I look upon my chain'ed watch,
A small crack in its glass,
So fragile, and ready to see
A time that once will last.

The Love Story

Once there was a little touch,
As soft as gentle light,
It held onto the heartstrings much,
E'en once it'd taken flight.

Once there was a little thought,
Though dangerous it be,
Was only that which can't be bought,
And makes it hard to see.

Once there was a silent hope,
Brought in at morning last;
It made a way for one to cope
With sadness of the past.

Once there was a whispered word
That shouted through the night,
And traveled o'er to one that heard—
For nothing stopped its might.

Once there was a quiet walk,
Though bubbling, two may be,
And soon the silence grew to talk
As he bent to a knee.

Once there was a happy girl
Who learned to love at last;
And nothing now could strike the world
Her love she held to fast.

Once there was a cloudy day
When sunshine came no more,
When children didn't laugh or play,
Yet then she felt once more.

Once there was an empty hour
When nothing moved or stilled;
But still she knew, above all pow'r,
A love that never killed.

"Between you and I"

Between you and I,
The story remains
Untold to the world
And hidden the pain.

Between you and I
Are days smiling bright,
Laughter together,
Your charm making right.

Between you and I
Are bitterness, strife,
Closed doors, empty words,
The end of a life.

Between you and I
Are heartache and pride,
Forgotten mem'ries,
And days when you lied.

Between you and I,
Forgiveness was made;
No time for regret
Of words then mislaid.

Between you and I,
A teardrop did fall;
Where your hand should touch,
There's nothing at all.

Between you and I,
Our story shall be
Days that never came,
Promise we'll not see.

Veritas

Words and lies are heavy things,
And surely made of stone,
They weigh you down and break apart
The place that they called home.

A Cry from a Lonely Heart

All the fellow mystics cry:
A heart was meant for two.
Before a page, the chapter ends,
But first, a love that's true.
Carrying a weight that binds,
Cryptic hearts will contain
Deadly arrows and careless hands,
Draining such love to pain.
Encroaching on this heart mine,
Eating at all our joy,
Feelings then torn with thoughtless words,
Forgetting it's a ploy.
Greet the hand with a gentle kiss,
Grounding a heart from clouds.
Heartless touch with a burning mark
Heating mem'ry that shrouds.
Ignited love starts too soon,
Ignoring when it counts.
Jesting made at what means the most,
Jilted, and tears as founts.
Killing soul, abandoned now—
Keep it so safe and sound.
Love is not meant for all heartbeats;
Loneliness, more eas'ly found.
Make safe the chapt' not yet read,
Mending the fence that's down,
Never open the wound to scar
Nostalgia's weary crown.
On dreary days, rains will come
Over our mirrored mood

Peering from heaven's glitt'ring beams,
Perfecting what it should.
Quest'ning hearts this mystery,
Quoting memories past,
Realizing light can come again,
Regaining what was cast.
Silver bands of fire and ice
Select the truest hand
'Til all is well in joyful homes,
Together, two hearts stand.
United books, unnamed tales,
Unbending what is true.
Venetian blue makes starry nights,
Vivid with light and hue.
Wat'ry eyes of pain no more,
Weary, their heads will rest;
Yielding quiet, their chapter ends,
Youthful, and found, and blest.

The Bracelet

Mirrored eyes now etched in fading stone:
Break from the gaze to hands now made alone.

All you feel, a sunlit frame,
An empty heart and shattered name,
When all you wished for was in vain,
And nothing will be the same.
You cry and scream, dashing hope,
And bravely cling to knotted rope,
Knowing the tie is fraying fast.
Hold your breath; t'will be the last.

Once you thought your self seemed true,
But now you are alone in view,
Wearing such shades of varied blue,
And darkness shrouds obscured hue.
Golden light in redded locks,
Stolen moments and thrilling talks—
Repeating always your mind's past.
Why think you this time will last?

Echoing, you can't contain
The strings' that shake and won't remain,
Shouting, "I loved you more!" in vain—
Hardened wood, your fragile frame.
Alas, child, you made to soar
These mountain dreams, your hope the core.
Your feathers flew to highest shore,
Falling now to rise no more.

Violent, fragile plumes will quake;
Your thoughts and body now will break.
Tied fast you are, as flames rise high
To vanished dreams that met sky.
They laugh at pain, at shed tear.
Lifeless float and embrace your fear.
Full eyes losing what was held dear,
Without feeling, none held near.

Awake from dreams and night's spite;
Be calm here in your needless fright!
Embrace the real and what is known;
Ponder these thoughts silent, alone.
Droplets line your cheeks to tend
The words that tell you love's an end.
Never release, there's none to mend
Where people tell you to bend.

Behind bars of bone, go, hide yourself
In mem'ries kept with a ring on a shelf.

One Question

One question remains,
Before you become "free,"
When you look back in time,
Will you think of me?

Understanding

No time can tell, no mind can know
What sorrow causes us to grow.
Pick up your bag, a heavy heart
Of shattered pieces torn apart.
"Away, away!" they cry at night,
Like a bird who wished for flight.
Summer's dream fades from view;
Has anyone yet thought of you?
Restless fears peak again;
Fixated hope can die then.
Those fears always follow close,
The quiet whispers of a ghost:
"Let me sleep, forever dream,
Until I see the morning's gleam."
But awake one does with tears, once more;
Mind aches, a heart still sore.
"Where's the end, my broken heart?
That people love to tear apart?"
"Apart?" they say, with confused eye,
"Why do you so frozen lie?"
Unknown to them, these weak hands,
Hoping only just to lend
A helpful word, a gift or two,
If only a 'turned glance from you.
Yet we watch them waste away,
Forgotten in the rush of days.
"Alone I shall forever be
How could anyone love me?"
For truth be told, they're loved by most
Though pushed away from those close.

These quiet, small habits dismay
Those who urge to mend one way.
So contained thoughts fix one's sleep,
And even more throughout the week.
Wishing someone to understand!
Gazing at life here on the land,
Sea, sky, and earth alike
Is a home, within our sight.
Hidden safe behind this lens,
She captured all with ink and pen.

Cloudy Thoughts

Swirling, blurring, blindly luring
Into thoughts so swiftly burning
Memories and endless night,
Broken wings dying for flight.
Walking, running, all now the same
Echoing thoughts of your lost name.
Time will pass, hist'ry doth say,
Yet I wait the day away.
Forrest frosts the empty breezes,
Rustle soundless, crushing leav'es.
Dreams left for others to tread
Their death is still mine to dread.
Washing, wasting, wishfully light
Until I no more hear goodnight.
Endless days and thoughtless walks
To myself my own voice talks.
Screaming, crying, breaking of pain
Only soothed by tears of soft rain.
Caring, longing, soothing eye,
By that hand, they will be dry.

Sleepwalk

Time stares like a hawk
walking from room to room.
                        It follows
with gleaming eyes.
Children laugh, and scream,
               play, and cry,
as I hold dried ink on pages not my own.
I sleep, and the owls
                     unresting
hoot at me in protest.
Their loosed feathers spin,
       hands on a clock turn.
And the blurred glass of silhouette
empties when it meets the dusty earth.
With the second law, the sun
        faithfully chiding,
               always reminding
that it sets with another day lost.
I am here, eyes darkened with days filled
to the brim with emptiness.
                      A jar of wasted breath
of things unsaid
              and words forlorn of thought.
And I stop with the hastening dawn,
purpose waking with sleepy thought
and I, soon dead, am alive again.

Numb

It's a stealthy pain,
like when fingertips exposed to
warm water burn
their nerves ending so much cold.
      It builds.
            The shock is there.
Why do tears wash away pain
           when pain invited them?
They stay too
like salt in a wound,
pride shattered with each drop.

When held at bay for too long,
let a cry in distant voice—
an echo no longer you—
make foreign ears.

It cries "I am lost"
          to empty space,
"why" to an empty room.

Broken, tearing, throaty sobs,
     pleading for relief,
         for the numbness to return.

The Flicker of the Candle

When darkness creeps into my skin,
Where fettered lays dusk and sin,
Fear will wait and stay awhile,
Baring its familiar smile.
The mist surrounds in shaggy coat,
A circlet tight about my throat,
To embed its thoughts, inspired
By my own mind's murky mire.
To tempt, to chill, to make its own
A fragile moment, in pain is sown.
Pressing dust back to its home
To mock at hope that's long since flown.
"But keep in view the candle's flame,
And the One who holds your name.
Don't look past at darkness deep,
Or let your mind a chance to peep
At what's beyond flick'ring light,
Your monster's goal for more than fright.
Wait for morning's dew once more,
And be bathed in new day's shore.
Before the night's drowning's past,
Your light's lot with Life's been cast."

Bottle Up My Tears

pain in a glass saved for a rainy day
filter downward as they stray
pat? And the drop hits
the floor where my heart sits
an ache tracing little glass
stairways where the feelings last
and in the spiral of my ear
the little place, sigh, here
a droplet of diamond thought
is a little shard caught
no pain like this is met
unfought, for all fear's kept
in glassy shards of rainlet meers
are found in my relented tears

Drops Like Blood

And the drops went down
in rivets and creases,
deep gashes and paths
with healing in their wake.
These brought none nor were sent
      by pain
           but instead
                chose to heal.
Such thirst was unknown
      until felt that first time.
Whole. How long had it been?
One small drop
      and it filled every gap.
No parting sorrow, no hidden treachery.
Simple, honest, good.
Without thought for want until it was there.
For once, the world shone
through that little drop.

Scars

It hurts to see pretty hands,
girls on their wedding day,
women with perfection,
while I
have scars—
little scratches across my skin.
Unhidden with powder
nor shaded with silk,
it will always be there.
Scarred.
Healed, but marked.

New Song

We spoke in lyrics of another's voice
in hopes, perhaps, that ours
be conveyed
and the other's
understood.

But not to be, we were lost in the notes,
forgetting that pages only contain
half the heart
that our tongue
and hand holds back.

Yet your hands were conniving
and mine slowly dying,
and you encouraged my fate
'til the sad symphony ended.

I heard yours a time ago,
the three quarter beat never reaching the forth.
A tease insisted.
A baited trap found.

Tiny Treasures

In this box I held my old life,
In this chest was found my past:
Tiny treasures on the table
That were soon gone at last.

Here I pondered all my memories,
Notes and dreams, no longer gone;
But these treasures on the table
Remind me I must end this song.

But let me hold them for a moment!
Let me mourn what once was mine!
Lest I forget the years they taught me
When my eyes no longer shine.

Yet, who am I to keep them?
Who am I who stands today?
These treasures lack their luster
Of farewells that autumn's day.

And to think this once defined me!
These words, and stones, and fears.
Now I'm spread upon a table,
A death of all I once held dear.

Thus, I sit and keep a memory
Of what I now must count as dead;
Tiny treasures on the table
Show of all that I have bled.

Sleep

Only in sleep do my dreams not wander,
My peace comes briefly in rest;
Only in silence, I fear no longer.
Could I find moments that last?

Only in dreams do my lips become free,
One little word do I say.
Only my worry will not let me be.
Will I at last find that day?

Only by lips can the heart fin'lly show,
When words break forth from their cage.
Only, will I be what I've let long grow,
My heart now a dark, torn page?

Only in time will I find this sought peace;
In dreams will my mind be sown.
Only my fear is left to be buried;
Then I will know I have grown.

From Clouds to Light

Days come when the sun does hide
Behind clouds that lost their delight
Their eerie glow consumed the night
A star sees, who gently sighed

Beyond hills, sunray imbued
Light on darkened hills colored long
And with the morning comes my song
For with each day love's renewed

As I walk that endless space
Of whisp'ring grass and lofty trees
Long-lost hopes, and vanishing seas
I know of a smiling face

Hearts disdain these hard-pressed days
Of no hope, joy, or endless peace
But only love which never ceased
Then I feel the warm sunrays

Quiet here, I intent watched
From my perch the sunset's slow fade
And with my thoughts its colors stayed
Soft, my heart its canvas touched

Without knowing, my eyes smile
Dwelling on these forever dreams
Not life's uncertain, tearing seams
For hurt only stays awhile

True, sadness joins happy tear
And bluebirds sing in morning light
As black to blue fades darkened night
The silver moon shows eyes clear

Around about, days are naught
And yet, to find a love that's true
The incredible sought, now knew
By Him alone I've been bought

Home

Autumn

Empty lay the broken stem,
Each golden leaf lay hushed;
Drifting to the softened glow,
The evening's breeze then brushed.

Dusting soft crisp covered grass,
Hide little motes of light
Finding hues here changing fast
From dreams now brought to sight.

Closing eyes and breathing slow,
Settle by death within.
Then embrace decay soon gone—
Such beauty betwixt sin.

Blues there stand amid the reds,
And pebbles mark the path—
Days once spent with two as one
And one with those that laugh.

Sighing spheres dip to the sea
While roses grace the sky;
One more page falls to the ground—
With me, forever lie.

Seasons

Swirling memories in far lost days—
A word, a thought, a smile—
With wonders, dreams, warm sunrays,
This time surpassed the miles.

When blustery days bring down the leaves,
Like feathers flashing light,
Their boughs sway in the eves—
So eerie in the night.

Glistening days of snowy path,
Snowflake crystals melt;
Joyful friends with eyes that laugh,
And on the grass they knelt.

But rainy days, they steal away
The snow so pure and white.
Replace with dark and mud-stained ground
The petal painted bright.

And while these glories glow with zest,
New life is born as well.
So, each mother feels truly blest,
Their songs indeed do tell.

And as the sky from blue to black
Transforms the clouds above,
The flash and drums seemly attack
Relentless, without love.

But heavens tears will wash away
The dull and sad of life
To enhance buds and blossoms more,
Enduring throughout strife.

So happy days go and come
Throughout life's days and years.
And whether life has smiles or none,
Remember happy tears.

Gifts and Thanks

You gave me the gifts of my hands
Nothing so great could I understand.
To write, to draw, to sing, to make—
All my works
                reflecting to create.
I'm thankful for speech, language too,
Communicating twixt me and You.
A gift unique, I can't fathom;
Of all your works, humans, you want them.
I'm touched by Your fingers truly;
All my life is blessed by You fully.
Never I'd wished to be loved so true—
For you forgive
                e'en when I fail you.
I'm blessed in the gifts of my hands,
Through voice, body, the creatures of land,
A mind to search these myst'ries bold,
A heart to care for people untold.
I thank Thee for the life You blessed;
In You I know I found perfect rest.
Undeserved I, You freely give.
And with bless'ed hope
                I freely live.

Lessons

And though you didn't mean
To teach me with this time,
These years brought many lessons
Left in this heart of mine.

For who would see falsehood?
The packages with string?
Such gifts appear a burden,
Though praises you did sing!

And who'd have ever thought?
And how could I confess?
These stories reek deception,
To relive caused distress.

My heart began to race
To think of hurt and pain,
So I closed doors around me
To shun such "friends" again.

Your arrogant nature,
Your pettiness and ploys,
Broke me as you'll never know
And fought to steal my joy.

Such future hopes were dashed,
And our friends you severed,
When you chose games and deceit
While we're left to weather

The effects of choices
That from us you then stole
And used our love to the last.
Selfishness was the goal.

But His love shone brighter
To keep my heart from stone.
And those who knew of friendship
Remind me I'm still known

By those who cared, loved us,
And chose to heal our hearts,
To move on from these lessons
That would tear us apart.

So, I will take mem'ries,
And start new days again.
These scars run deep inside now,
But His covered o'er sin.

Prayers

Lord, help me to forgive like You;
Soften my heart, please.
Let me know Your love is true,
And cherish Yours with ease.

Lord, help me to return these gifts
As Your means on earth,
Serving those who love me not
And seeing all they're worth.

Lord, help me show a love like Yours
In these days of mine.
Thinking of the other first
And care for them like Thine.

Lord, help me have a patient heart
As I walk this life,
Learning to be still and know,
And save me from my strife.

Thoughts of Remembrance

Falling softly on my ear,
Gently comes for me to hear,
Reminiscing thoughts, inspire
My dreams and my heart's desire;
And closing thoughts to end my days,
The sunbeams pour in countless rays.
My journey past changed future path,
Bring joy, sorrow, tears, and laugh.
But nostalgia now keeps me awake
And pleasant thoughts my mind to make.
Smiling heart, and thoughts made clear,
I left to ponder what was dear.
Closing eyes in shades of blue,
My wandering mind thought of you.

April Nights

Wonderful world of empty space—
A card, a ring, a stone—
On mossy stump, I find my place
In silent woods alone.

Racing up the slippery rocks,
Or keys both sharp and flat,
My heart then skipped once at the top
But descends like a cat.

Alone, remain quiet here, as
If something might happen;
But then, the future is unclear,
And soft eyes will dampen.

Then winter brings windy embrace,
The candle flinches, dies,
Taking the strength from warm'ed gaze
And welcome of cold eyes.

Before I fall asleep tonight—
A touch, a tear, a smile—
Is how I think of you, my sight,
Nostalgic all the while.

Just Because

Simple phrases, loving words,
The time to sing and dance,
My wand'ring thoughts alight the winds,
And gently, a glance.

Peaceful thought remembered by
A dream that's yet to come,
Softly passing open boughs—
Waiting's hard for some.

Medleys waken on the dawn,
A new day comes again;
Hopes follow at windowpane,
And returns a friend.

Day One

I waited until midnight,
But you left before twelve;
I wanted one more minute,
And you left me on a shelf.
And though all tried to warn
In the partings, words, and years,
I held to the last second
To embrace all their fears.
So I crumbled in the moments
That etched into my skin,
For you moved onto freedom
And I made walls within.
My fettered heart lay shattered,
Coating walls with pain,
Yet you chose to break my heart
On a New Year's Eve again.
But he made sure to replace
Your pained mem'ries with love.
And now I watch each year renew
With white wings of a dove.

The Wall

Hiding behind a corner,
So that I couldn't see,
Was yet one more surprise
Waiting just for me.
I had tried to push the wall,
I'd tried to go around,
But all of my hurry
Left me never found.
I ignored the wall a time,
My cuts and bruises raw,
In my attempts to scale
Things I shunned but saw.
I thought that if I maybe
Lost the light I had,
That I'd not be lonely
And I would be glad.
Instead, I found a small room
So dark, I surely lost
All my awe and wonder
With myself the cost.
Then I left it just to find
More heartache, loss, and pain,
Retracing all my steps
To sorrow again.
Thus, I sat in hollow tears,
My life a shallow mess,
Red from hurt and anger—
Broken and hopeless.
Then folded hands, bended knees,
Tried just so hard to pray

That instead of rushing
I'd still, wait, and stay.
"Stay?" asked I. No, surely not.
I'm not the patient type.
But wait I did and learned
The clear way of life.
Then I found more that I lacked—
Forgiveness, joy, and peace—
Which needed a place, and
In place every piece.
Then I found the wall so small,
Not rugged or so steep;
A bud grew at its bed
For my heart to keep.
I kept it as crept the days—
Behind, as well, before—
Stopping when I had found
Life with nothing more.
Peace came first, then mercy's heart,
Then joy and happiness.
I found with contentment,
One finds blessedness.
Then a chance with fate in mind
Came on that sunny day
When through the wall, I found
You, who came to stay.

...and then I met you

with wonderful thoughts
and non-stop mouth;
you with the books and stories,
and no idea left unshared.
You made me laugh,
held my hand,
pushing me on the precipice of tears
that I did not want to cross,
moving me anyway,
holding me fast.
I looked to you
and saw a smile
a little smirk, a little tease;
love woven within.
I saw eyes—
a mix of earth and sky—
and wished I could look longer.
You were not perfect
and still are not.
Your past
as inked as mine.
That's what made you right.
For when I met you,
you made me
remember
myself.
And for once,
I felt complete.

My Poem

You were the poem I couldn't write
I tried to fill you in
    with ink, paper, and words
        all of it leaving traces down
            your perfect skin
Then I realized
    you are
        skin and bones
            muscle and heart
I felt it as my finger traced   every inch of you

Nothing I said could describe
Nothing I wrote could compile
None of my creations were you
    and that was all that was perfect
Because you… skin, scars, and heart
            were you
I couldn't change that, and I loved you for it
Every inch of you I loved
I could not write you, because you were a story
I couldn't tell
    until you told it, entrusted it, to me
        It is our secret.
Now your fingers leave traces of new words
            on my skin
and only your heart reads them

Moondance

Darkness covers, the moon barely woke,
A simple caress across water spoke
A smile, a touch of wind to its face
Gentle movement to tease and to grace.
Watch light trace down, and shivers ensue;
A stirring response of deep eyes to move.
Up goes the cloth with the stars to alight
Skin in the glow of the stirring sight:
One heart to own, now over the wall,
Embracing movement kept still then gave all—
All of self, together, body and soul,
The world in a moment, a self full.
A kiss soft like the moon to the sea
Whose waves drove back embrace so sweet, so free.
No fear crept into the heart still so frail
On this broadsheet was trust like a sail.
So strong, so sure, a bit reckless, true,
With eyes as deep as the night sea is blue.
The moon then brought waves now begging release,
Collapsing as one, harbored in peace.
Bliss can't describe what ignorance begs,
But this love unleashed washed over the dregs.
Once empty, unfilled, the wrong ones to drink
Greedy to take, never stopped to think
Of storms unsettled, and left behind
To steer to safekeeping, solely to find.
Here the past faded, the morning made new,
And sea to moon was clearly in view.

Red Nights

Now draw me up, and hold me in
Sew me back together again
Then touch my skin this gentle way
Kissing my hair while smiles play
Forget the time, the evening's late
My heart is in a messy state
Tracing my curves, up and unwound
Discover me in new ways found
Then hold me tight, don't let me go
And whisper softly, nice and slow
Before sunlight begins to creep
Into my soul I'll let you peek
So come here close, for when you're near
No shadowed past brings me to fear
And when the sun awakes the day
Within your heart will mine then stay
No words, worries, action askew
Could ever now part me from you

Twined Souls

Naked soul deeper than skin
you unbury.
      Your touch
      unravels my fears
as you sew shut the wounds,
the tears of my fabric soul—
frayed, patchy, unhealed.
My threaded past a web,
confounding heart in
the body's mistakes.
But the veil drops
and you see me
unhindered.
Yet you choose to touch
        this scarred skin.
I tried to cover with cloth,
     woven lies.
   Instead,
hands pulled away the mask,
the search over with a touch.
You found beauty in ashes.
I found love unrobed,
   unhindered,
   true.

Inkhorn Mornings

Balanced to the brim to spill
over and onto the page thoughts
so ready to flow, so hesitant
        Don't touch!
                I will forget.
My train left at yester week;
the stage has since departed.
The sea rolls, the surface blank
And I, so rapid fires the pulse
empty the buckets and
        It splashes. Too soon?
I won't dwell
               that date has passed.
Shaky fingers engulf the quilled ink
pouring the lifeblood so dark.
Down it rolls to the left
                    It's done.
The pail rests on the floor
and my footsteps echo in its walls.

Animated Lines

I love the smell of
graphite
        and dead trees
pressed, cold, thick
blank, waiting to be made
        Alive again.
I love the sound of
a sharpened point
        grinding against
        a rough surface
darkening to make bold
taking away to show life.
I love the feel of a wrist
        bending to and fro
        back and forth
the curve found only in
        the animate
            kept frozen on a sheet.

I love the smell of
        dust and ashes, and ground life
waiting to be carved
waiting to be sculpted
        on a canvas
        of dead trees, and graphite.

This Old House

The knobs are loose
The floor a wreck
And nary a wall with poise
The door frames tilt
The windows lilt
And e'ry small step makes noise

The cracks hide high
They reach down low
But where do they begin?
The lights shed none
Of this, I'm done
And yet I'm stuck within

The couch is cold
There drafts come in!
But what am I to do?
The furnace's set
The basement's wet
And surely not with dew

The street's too close
The yard dismayed
My patience wearing thin
Each stone is chipped
Each wire clipped
All evidence of sin

And yet I wait
Though not too long
For a moment's waiting past
My thanks is sure
I can endure
'Til House is gone at last

Church Bells

In the dusk and in the quiet,
I can hear the bells of light.
Underneath the cloudy moon flit
And the snow to keep from sight,
I can hear the bells still ringing,
Quietly, their tones are singing.
Skipping through the frost, they splinter
'Cross the dells in midst of winter.

Though this time will be forgotten,
In a day, or hour, no more,
And the silence soon is broken,
Like a wave upon the moor,
I will rest within the memory
When I felt such peace inside me,
Listening still, and watching silent,
Your faint bells upon the quiet.

In a moment, I will stir then
To my tasks, the evening calls.
For the rest I long has since been
Ended like the snowy falls.
But as dusky hue surrounds me,
I will think back on so fondly
All of your sweet peals far away
And keep them close 'til break of day.

Little One

I tried for days,
Between spaces and moments,
From the first time I thought,
Then the hour I almost knew,
To when you were more than an idea,
And you became a reality—
So small, so fragile,
      I forgot some days,
And pushed through some others.
I prayed, and thought, and hoped,
          And I barely dared
To let myself reach too much.
For I realized, little one,   that I am afraid.
So very afraid, little one.

My fear started in a small place,
Creeping in so many years ago,
But I never really forgot it.
And I'm so scared, little one,
What the reality of you would mean.

What if you cry?
Your fears are so much bigger than I.
And I, so little in strength,
Cannot help you?
What if you, precious one,
Do not want me?
         My voice, my touch, my smell,
Foreign to you, though part of who you are.
What then, little one?

My beautiful one, what if I don't see?
Your precious face, I saw in a mirror,
                And a little tear fell.
I didn't know your face, but I wanted, so much,
Little one, to hide you from the prods.
I wanted to keep you safe.
Lull you with hymns and words.
But what if, little one,
What if my love is not enough?

I'm so scared, little one,
    That I won't be
        Everything you hope,
            Everything you need.
                The one you want.

(Please don't let me be too broken!)

I'm so scared, little one,
That I won't know how to love you.
That scares me.
What if I cannot, little one?

Will you be patient with me
            As I with you
                'Til we learn each other?
These lessons are bigger than us both.
Precious one. Forgive me.
I love you so much, little one.
Will you love me too?

New Life

It's like the first of winter,
With blooms just coming up,
The grass turns brown to greener,
And buds make little cups.
The dew and sun-graced petals
Turn drops of rain to light,
And crystals slowly dripping
Made goodbye kiss to sight.
I watched as trees grew taller,
And a bird made her nest
So safe from wakeful creatures—
Her young ones she wished best.
Then altered rose the morning
In once forgotten blue;
And I began to see as
These eyes did soften new.
For life had joy and meaning,
The sun and moon their place,
The players make their movements,
And hearts could return grace.
This life is more than one now,
Such hope and peace it holds,
As mornings start with laughter
And new promise unfolds.
The sunset brought the starlight,
And petals said goodnight;
I feathered o'er my darlings—
Their life now makes mine bright.

Grace

I sit in the nursery,
Here rocking to and fro,
Waiting for the moment
Of peace, its face to show.

I look at my gray shirt,
Now covered in your drool,
And wonder to the day
When I'll wear something new.

I'd burned all the baked goods
And measured in wrong ways
While you emptied cupboards
And had so much to say.

I might have yelled just once
And cried out to the void
As I picked up the laundry
For weeks I did avoid.

I failed myself today,
Just as the week before.
With no dinner cooking,
And dad came through the door.

You saw my anger showing,
But still gave no complaint,
Showing me your picture
Made on the wall with paint.

Sighing in that moment
I put away your toys.
For what else could I do
To drown out all the noise?

Noise of all my making
As I busied my days
In tasks, crafts, and cleaning
Until the evening rays.

Then you toddled softly
Into my arms again;
And my sin crept between
To push my heart within.

But grace found its moment,
And you opened my heart
Holding me in chaos
That would tear us apart.

Now I rock in quiet
While you sleep in my arms
For me to see clearly
That you hold all life's charms.

I wear something new now—
So small and fragile be—
A thing of my creation
Who somehow still loves me.

Smiling in that moment,
My toe then kicked a toy.
It'd be there tomorrow,
A work that brings me joy.

But these times won't linger,
And snuggles soon will cease;
Growing beyond my arms,
You'll seek from me no peace.

Tightly now I hold you,
Your mouth parted so small.
As I stare to your face,
How could I part at all?

Laundry still is waiting,
The meals still unprepared,
But I won't miss my world
That you now with me shared.

I rock you back and forth
With stolen moment's peace,
Thankful for your bright grace
And teaching me to cease.

Midnight Visits

This candlelight cannot define
Your sparkling windows small.
A tiny touch, a start'ling glance,
And wonderment of all.

I wake to find your waiting face,
A little moon to me.
My view is not of skyscrapers—
I'd trade it all for thee.

I watch your breath fade into peace,
Such trust in me you show.
A glimpse into His world I see;
His love for us I know.

Last Night's Waking

Your whispers wake me softly
As I steal toward your room,
Where your steady little breaths
Say sleep is ready soon.

Your fingertips lay gently,
And snuggled all around
A blanket waits there for you,
So close and quickly found.

I know I should be sleeping,
But watching you tonight
My heart starts beating faster,
I smile with delight.

Such love can fill me fully,
This joy o'er brims my heart!
While watching you sleep soundly,
How can I now depart?

Your dreams must be so peaceful
Knowing that we are there.
I wish to hold you closer,
But all I do is stare.

Stare, and think back fondly
On moments, days, and years,
As I watched you grow quickly,
Learning without a fear.

My child, I hold you always,
Though you squirm from my arms.
My heart is ever with you
As you learn from life's harms.

But as I watch you dreaming
Of all your future days,
I wish to keep you here now
Before come new sun rays.

For time passed by too quickly,
Though you are hardly grown;
I just need one more moment,
One day for love that's shown.

Your little life brings beauty—
In all its sinfulness—
For echoed here I see love
As such God holds for us.

So let me stay this moment
As your breaths rise and fall
To hold onto these mem'ries
Before the morning's call.

For I held your small fingers,
Those toes, and eyes so bright,
Within, and still beside me;
Your face is my delight!

I cherish all these blessings,
Of days filled up with fun,
Of snuggles in the moonlight
When life's sad moments run.

My arms once held you tightly
As you fell sound asleep.
Then I was the way alone
You found your dreams so deep.

But now I watch from doorframes,
And sneak close by your bed,
Just to know you're safe and sound,
Brush kisses on your head.

You may be one day older,
And I one day behind,
But I won't forget moments
That make this life divine.

So snuggle in your blankets,
As you once clung to me,
And know that my love runs deep
As midnight in the sea.

The moonlight kissed you softly,
As I stood near your room,
Breathing soft just one more prayer
For peace 'til morning soon.

About the Author

Madelyn Rose Craig is an author from Southeast Michigan. Madelyn began writing at a young age, but her passion for writing and sharing her work grew when she was 16. To date, her works have included essays on apologetics, short stories, and poetry. She earned a bachelor's degree in English and Art from Concordia University, Ann Arbor, in 2016. In 2020, she published her first book: *Names, Nations, and the New Testament.* Madelyn is wife to an adoring husband, mother to a curious daughter and smiley son, and owner of a rambunctious Labrador. If she is not writing or reading, she is probably on a walk with her family, painting, or playing guitar. For more information about the author and her work, check out her website madelynrosecraig.com.

www.ingramcontent.com/pod-product-compliance
Lightning Source LLC
LaVergne TN
LVHW011848060526
838200LV00054B/4222